On Our Way to English®

Student
Book

Contents

Unit 1 Paired Stories

1

What Can We Do Today?

By Jason Powe

2

Our Big Move

By Wendy Lee

Unit 2 Paired Stories

Nonfiction Vocabulary Readers

3

What Is This?

By Emma Riba

4

Time to Dress!

By Cristina Moreno

Unit 3 Paired Stories

Nonfiction Vocabulary Readers

5

Can You Find the Shape?

By John Wu

6

What Signs Say

By Jason Powe

Unit 4 Paired Stories

Nonfiction Vocabulary Readers

7

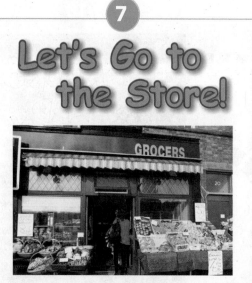

Let's Go to the Store!

By Daniela Torres

8

Please Come to Dinner!

By Regina Beaumont

Unit 5 Paired Stories

9

I Want a Pet

By Candy Rodo

10

By Megan Linke
Illustrated by David Arnau

11

Where Animals Live

By Marc Riba

12

By Megan Linke
Illustrated by Pam López

Unit 6 Paired Stories

13

What's in a Year?

By Javier Sánchez

14

RAINY DAY

By Megan Linke
Illustrated by Pam López

15

The Four Seasons

By Candy Rodo

16

SUMMER

By Megan Linke
Illustrated by Pam López

Unit 7 Paired Stories

| Nonfiction Vocabulary Readers | Fiction Readers |

17

Compare and Contrast

By Catalina Martí

18

The Three Little Pigs

Traditional Tale
Illustrated by Moni Pérez

19

Let's Grow Flowers!

By Emma Riba

20

THE LITTLE SEED

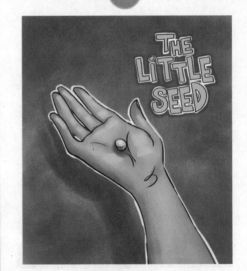

By Megan Linke
Illustrated by Pam López

Unit 8 Paired Stories

Nonfiction Vocabulary Readers	Fiction Readers

21

Safety First!

By Kevin Adkins

22

Little Red Riding Hood

Traditional Tale
Illustrated by Eva Sánchez

23

Let's Go!

By Eduardo Casas

24

THE BIG RACE

By Megan Linke
Illustrated by Pam López

My ABC Pages

A B C D

E F G

H I J K

L M N O P

Q R S

T U V

W X

Y Z

Aa

A B

Cc

s m u j m
W a c i j
u c r C l c g
t c f c s C e
h c C C c C i
b M c c
A B C D

D v d
g d D
d g p
e c

Ee

E	e	e	e	E
e	a	C	b	c
e	e	E	E	E
e	C	b	b	c
E	e	e	e	E

A B C D E F

8

Ff

F
e
f

f
o L
f f

f

u
f l

l
f

G g

A B C D E F G H

10

H	u	e	P	h
h	p	u	e	h
H	h	H	H	h
h	u	p	e	H
H	u	P	e	h

Ii

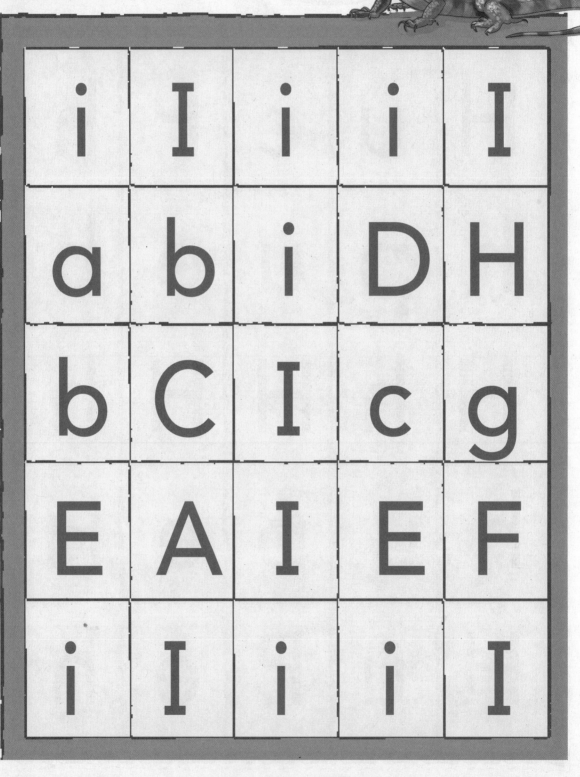

i	I	i	i	I
a	b	i	D	H
b	C	I	c	g
E	A	I	E	F
i	I	i	i	I

A B C D E F G H I J

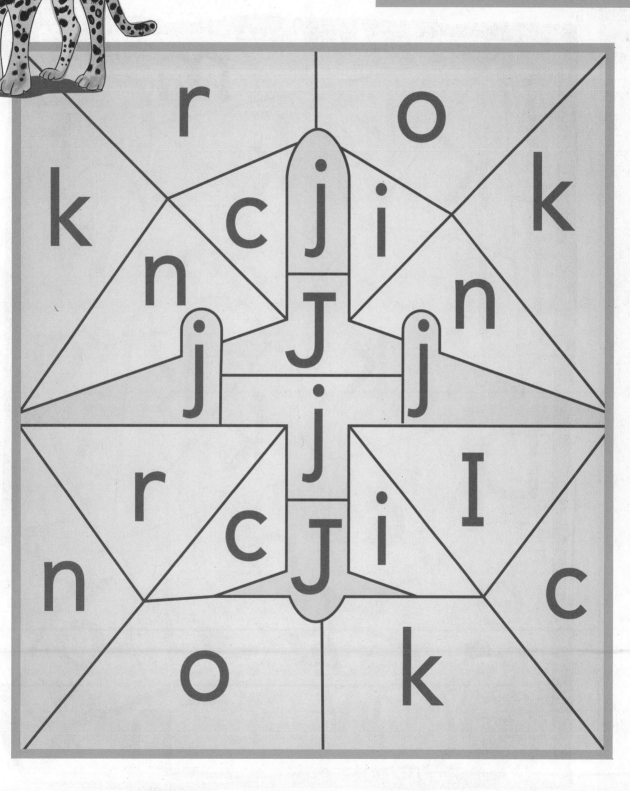

Kk

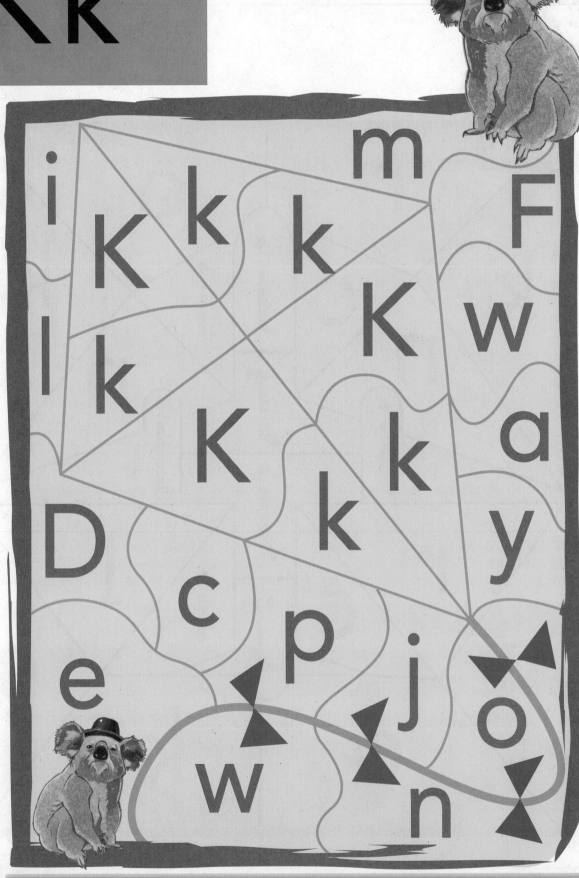

A B C D E F G H I J K L

14

Mm

B z z z

M

m

D

d

M

m

D z M m m

m

m

m

m

m

M

A B C D E F G H I J K L M

16

N

Oo

A B C D E F G H I J K L M

Qq

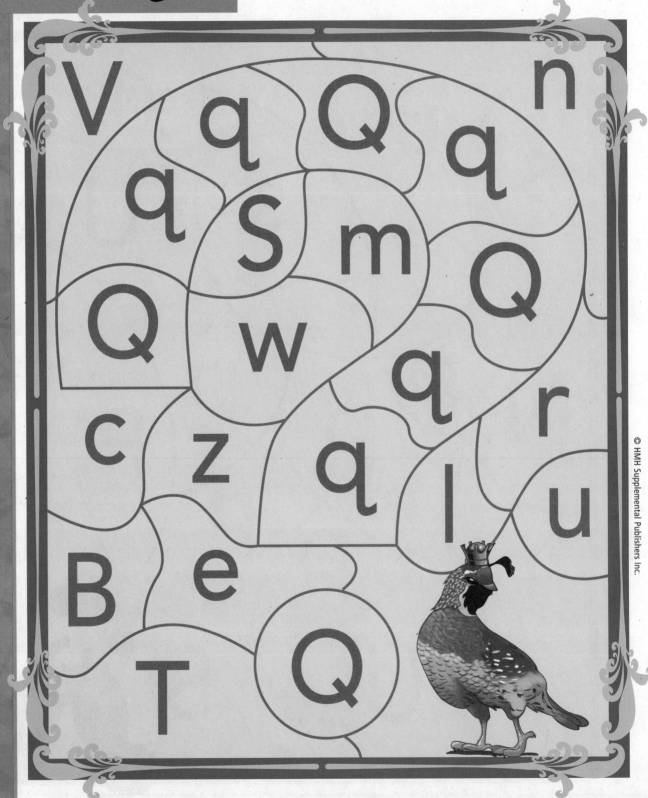

A B C D E F G H I J K L M

Rr

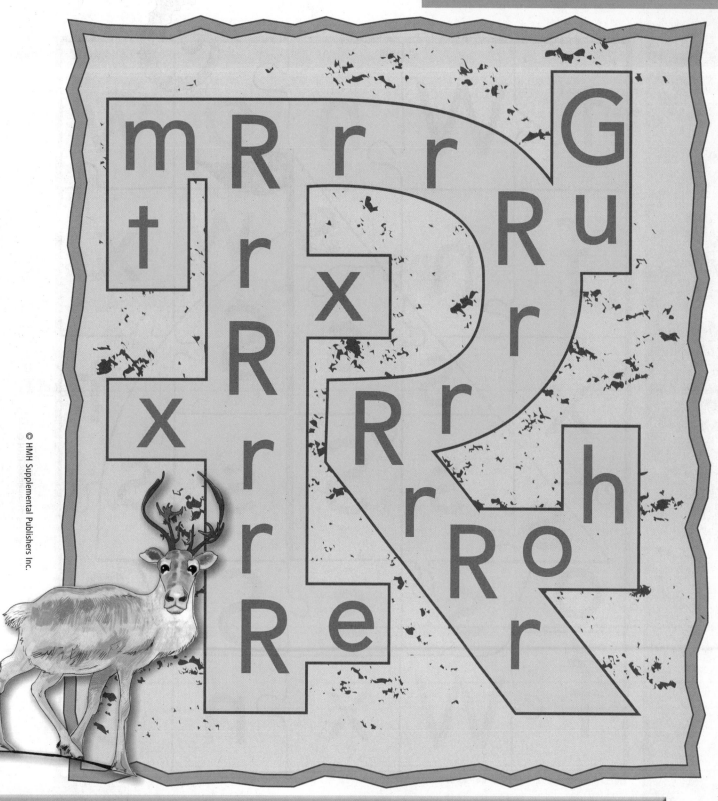

N O P Q R

Ss

A B C D E F G H I J K L M

T	t	t	t	T
B	s	T	s	r
s	s	t	r	b
r	s	T	r	B
b	s	t	r	s

N O P Q R S T

U u

A B C D E F G H I J K L M

Vv

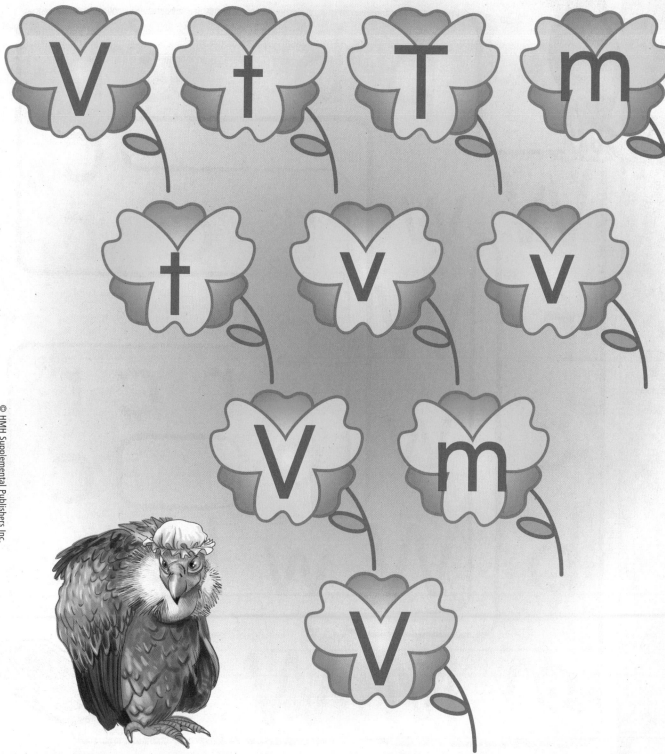

N O P Q R S T U V

Ww

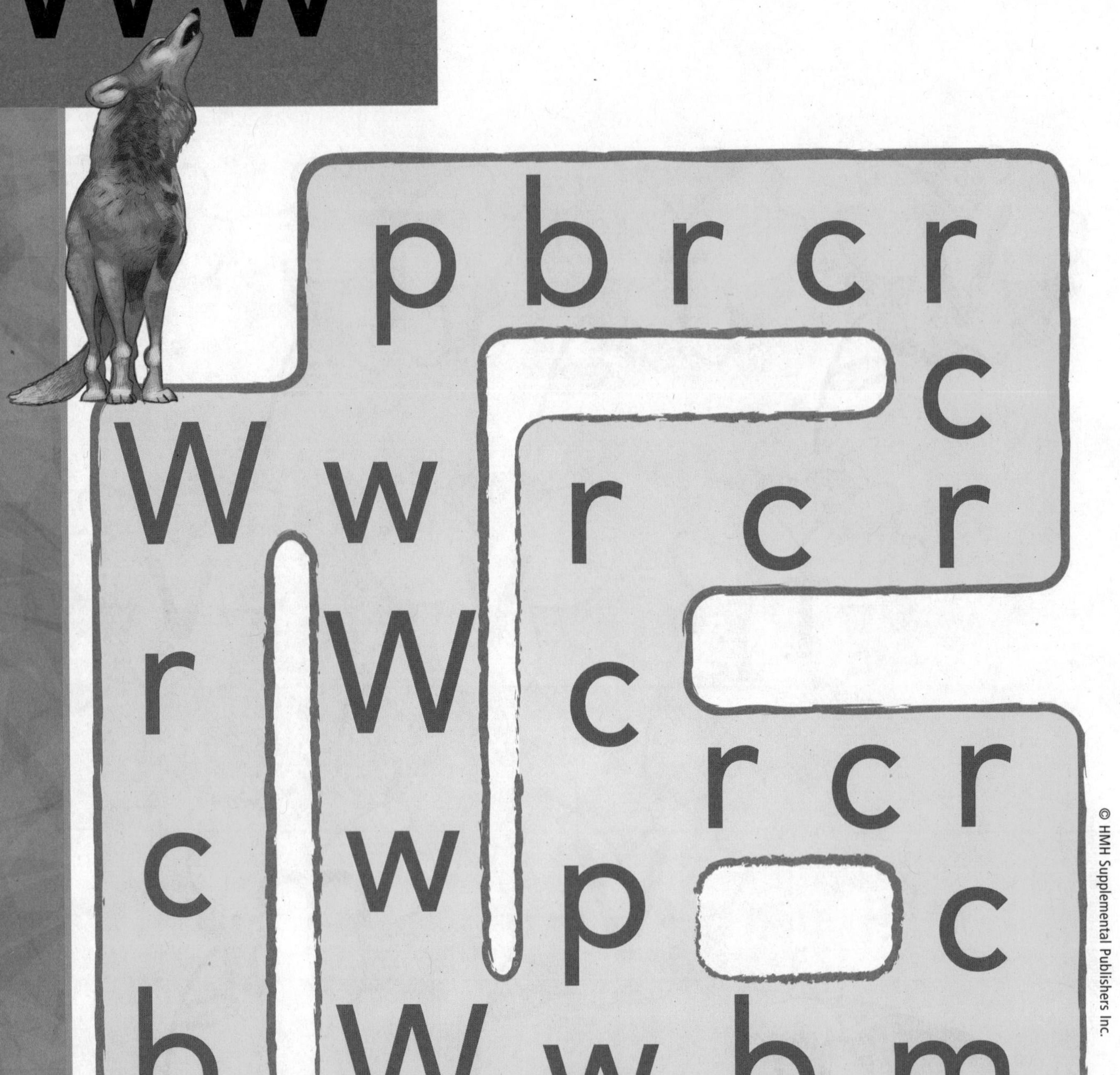
p b r c r
c
W w r c r
r W c
r c r
c w p c
b W w b m
m M W w

A B C D E F G H I J K L M

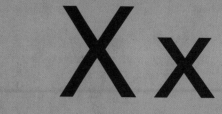

N O P Q R S T U V W X

Yy

A B C D E F G H I J K L M

28

N O P Q R S T U V W X Y Z

At School

The **BIG** Question

What do we see and do at school?

☐ What are you doing now?

☐ What do you see?

☐ Who is sitting next to you?

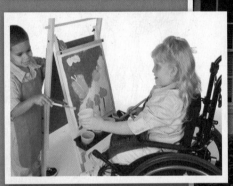

About School!

1. What do you see at school?

books

friends

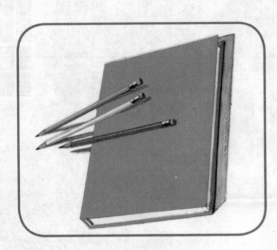

notebook

desk

2. What can you do?

I can paint.
I like to paint!

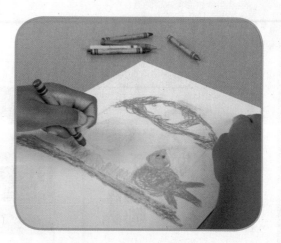

I can color.
I like to color!

I can read.
I like to read!

I can play.
I like to play!

Say **more!** Look for this mark: !
Why do we need it?

book

school

wonder

today

tomorrow

first

Talk about the words.

friends

play

new

paint

color

read

 Say a word. Act it out.

Paired Readings

Get ready to read.

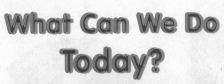

What Can We Do Today?

By Jason Powe

Our Big Move

By Wendy Lee

Talk About It

Look at the covers.
Talk about what you see.

- Do you see  ?

- Do you see  ?

Check Understanding

What Can We Do Today?

By Jason

A. Listen. Complete the chart.

1. I know about school.	☺	😐	☹
2. I understand this story.	☺	😐	☹

B. Answer the questions.

1. Who is writing?

 ☐

 ☐

2. Who is wondering?

 ☐

 ☐

Check Understanding

A. Listen to the story.
Complete the chart.

1. I know these words.	😊	😐	😩
2. I understand the story.	😊	😐	😩

B. Answer the questions.

1. Which is the old school?

☐ ☐

2. Who are the new friends?

☐ ☐

Interview

Get to know people in class.
Ask what their favorite color is.

Ask a Friend		Ask a Teacher	
red ☐	orange ☐	red ☐	orange ☐
yellow ☐	green ☐	yellow ☐	green ☐
blue ☐	purple ☐	blue ☐	purple ☐

 Switch roles! Let a friend ask you.

Writing

Listen. Look. Complete the sentence.

_____

- -

I _____ at school.

Progress Check

Look at the picture. Check the word.

1.

☐ tomorrow

☐ paint

☐ first

2.

☐ paint

☐ color

☐ new

3.

☐ play

☐ read

☐ today

All About Me

The **BIG** Question

What do you know about yourself?

☐ How old are you?

☐ What color is your hair?

☐ What can you do?

43

1. I can put on my _____.

pants

shirt

socks

shoes

2. I can point to my _____.

nose

ears

eyes

mouth

 Say **more!** Each person is different. What makes you special?

ear

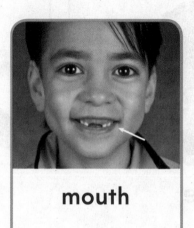

mouth

nose

put on

pants

shirt

Pick a word. Say it.
Find the object.

sock

shoe

dress

person

different

eye

 Pick a word. Say it.
Find the object.

Paired Readings

Get ready to read.

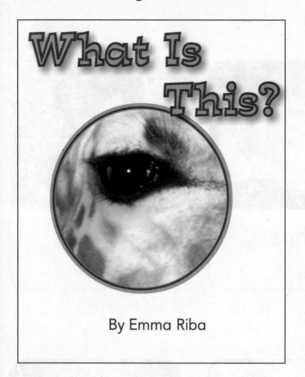

By Emma Riba

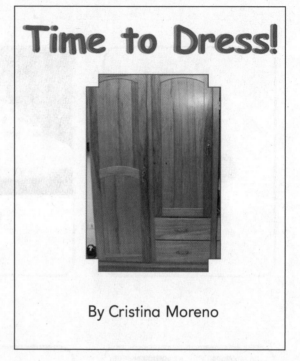

By Cristina Moreno

Flip through the books.
Draw what you see.

Check Understanding

What Is This?

By Emma Riba

A. Listen to the story.
   Complete the chart.

1. I know about animals.	🙂	😐	☹️
2. I understand this story.	🙂	😐	☹️

B. Check the right animal.

1.

2.

49

Marco Monkey

M

m

moon

mouse

mask

map

mop

marbles

Check Understanding

A. Listen to the story.
Complete the chart.

1. I know these words.	😊	😐	☹️
2. I understand the story.	😊	😐	☹️

B. Show the order from the story. Write 1 or 2.

1.

2.

Susie Seahorse

sandwich

sailboat

salad

sunset

saddle

socks

Writing

Listen. Look. Complete the sentence.

_____

- -

I have _____.

Progress Check

A. Check the letter that matches.

		r	m	s
1.	M	☐	☐	☐
		Z	F	S
2.	s	☐	☐	☐
		s	f	j
3.	S	☐	☐	☐
		M	S	W
4.	m	☐	☐	☐

B. Review the letters.

What letter? What sound?
M s S m

Progress Check

Look at the picture. Check the word.

1.

- ☐ nose
- ☐ shirt
- ☐ ear

2.

- ☐ sock
- ☐ nose
- ☐ eye

3.

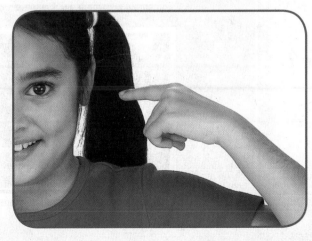

- ☐ mouth
- ☐ ear
- ☐ shoe

All Around Me

The **BIG** Question

How is a community like a family?

☐ **Who works in your community?**

☐ **What does your neighborhood look like?**

☐ **What do you see on your way to school?**

132 Park St.

LEA'S ROOM

DAY	GOAL	TIME	✓
1	SWIM	20 MIN.	😊
2	CHORES	30 MIN.	😊
3	SWIM	20 MIN.	😊
4	CHORES	30 MIN.	😊
5	SWIM	20 MIN.	
6	CHORES	30 MIN.	
7	SWIM	20 MIN	

57

About What's Around Us!

1. What is on your street?

cars

signs

2. What is in your house?

rooms

my family

What place do you like best?

3. What shapes are all around you?

triangle

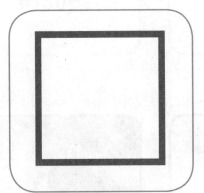

square

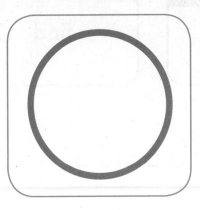

circle

Say **more!** Shapes help us.
Tell how.

59

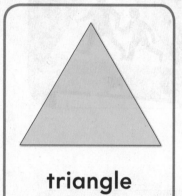

triangle

circle

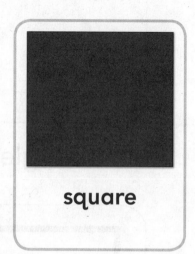

square

help

lost

find

Pick a word. Draw a picture.

sign

street

best

room

house

place

 Pick a word. Talk about it.

Antonia Alpaca

A A

a

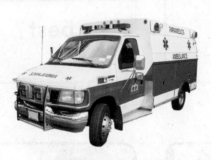

ambulance

apples

antlers

ants

ax

alphabet

Paired Readings

Get ready to read.

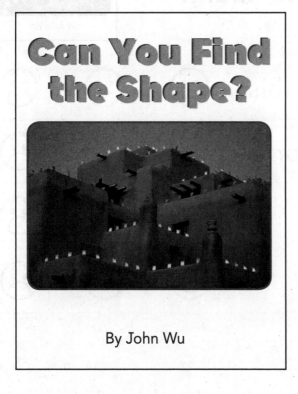

Can You Find the Shape?

By John Wu

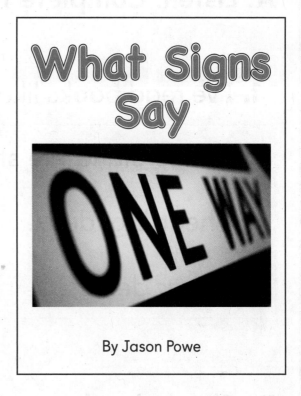

What Signs Say

By Jason Powe

Flip through the books.
Talk about the shapes you see.

Talk with your teacher.
How are these stories the same?

Check Understanding

Can You Find the Shape?

By John Wu

A. Listen. Complete the chart.

1. I've read books like this.	😊	😐	😦
2. I understand the story.	😊	😐	😦
3. I hear big ideas.	😊	😐	😦
4. I hear details.	😊	😐	😦

B. Check the shapes you see in the pictures.

1.

triangle ☐   circle ☐

2.

circles ☐   squares ☐

64

Felicia Flamingo

F

f

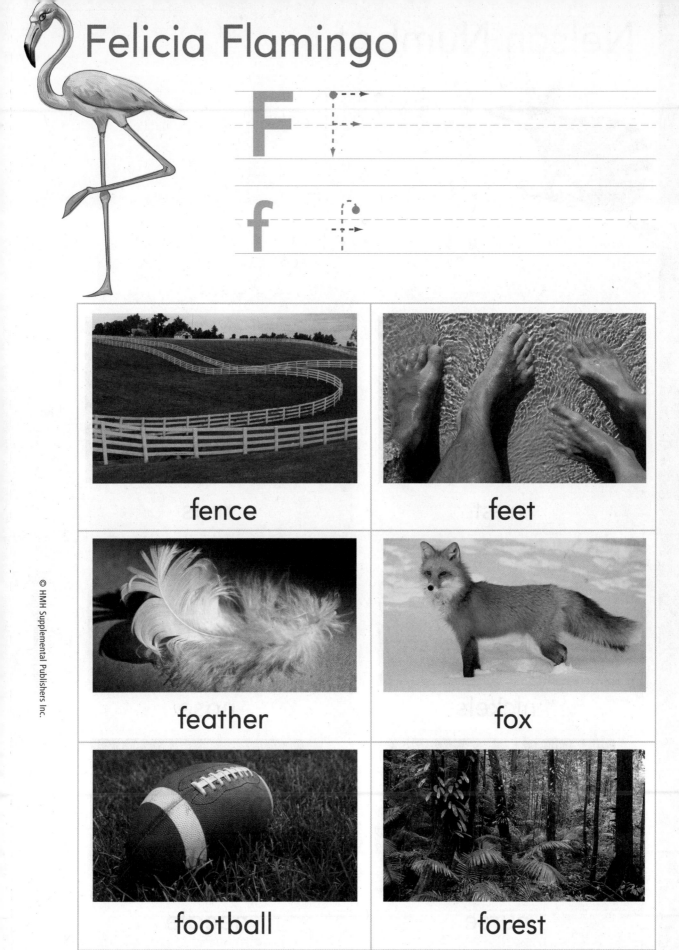

fence

feet

feather

fox

football

forest

Nelson Numbat

N N

n n

nest

nuts

nickels

nose

nurse

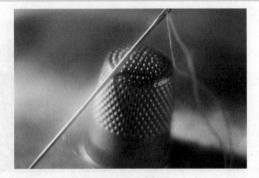

needle

Latifa Lemur

leaves

lion

lamb

ladder

lizard

lake

Coco Cobra

castle

carrots

cows

canoe

digital camera

cat

Check Understanding

A. Listen to the story.
Complete the chart.

1. I know these words.	😊	😐	😧
2. I understand the story.	😊	😐	😧

B. Match the shapes with the words.

1.　　　　　　　　　STOP　　　　　　MAIN

☐　　　　　　☐

2.　　　　　　　　　ONE WAY　　　　SLOW

☐　　　　　　☐

Benito Bull

B B
b b

balloons

bubbles

bear

bus

butterfly

bananas

Writing

Complete the sentence.

A community is _____.

Progress Check

Check the letter that matches.

		n		c		m	
1.	N	☐		☐		☐	
2.	f	F ☐		L ☐		B ☐	
3.	S	g ☐		s ☐		c ☐	
4.	C	c ☐		a ☐		s ☐	
5.	l	B ☐		F ☐		L ☐	

B. Review the letters.

What letter? What sound?

A f N s M

© HMH Supplemental Publishers Inc.

Progress Check

Look at the picture. Check the word.

1.

- ☐ square
- ☐ place
- ☐ triangle

2.

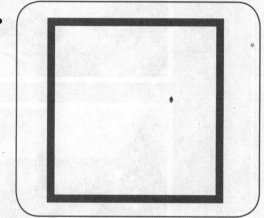

- ☐ best
- ☐ square
- ☐ circle

3.

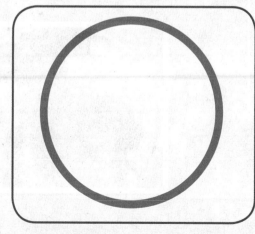

- ☐ triangle
- ☐ circle
- ☐ room

Let's Eat

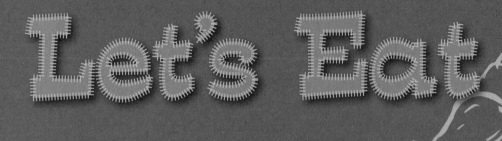

The **BIG** Question

Why is eating healthy food important?

☐ What foods are healthy?

☐ What did you eat today?

☐ What is your favorite food?

75

1. What meal do you like best?

breakfast

lunch

dinner

snacks

What else do you like to eat?
What do you like to drink?

2. What do you like to do?

I like to shop.

I like to make food.

I like to set the table.

I like to wash up.

 Tell why.
I like to shop because I like to eat.

eat

store

food

breakfast

lunch

dinner

Pick a word. Draw a picture.

count

make

full

set

table

drink

 **Say a word. Act it out.**

Ollie Otter

octopus

on

otter

oxen

omelet

olive

Paired Readings

Get ready to read.

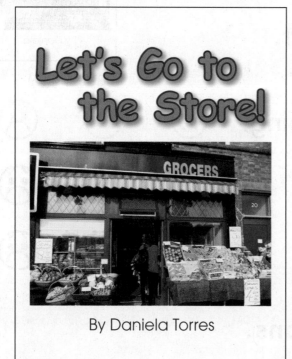

By Daniela Torres

By Regina Beaumont

Talk About It

Look through the books.
Talk about what you see.

- Do you see  ?

- Do you see  ?

81

Check Understanding

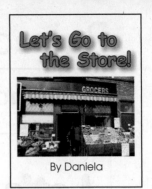

Let's Go to the Store!

By Daniela

A. Listen to the story.
Complete the chart.

1. I know about shopping.	☺	😐	☹
2. I hear big ideas.	☺	😐	☹
3. I hear details.	☺	😐	☹

B. Answer the questions.

1. What do we eat?

eggs

☐

list

☐

2. What do we drink?

fish

☐

milk

☐

Ping Panda

P P

p p

parade

panda

pumpkins

piano

paint

pizza

Hector Hippo

H

h

horse

hats

hammer

helicopter

house

hippo

Tarak Tiger

tiger

team

telephone

tire

turkey

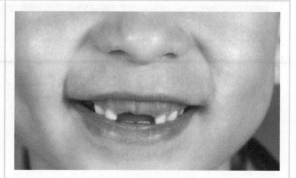
teeth

Rekki Reindeer

R R

r r

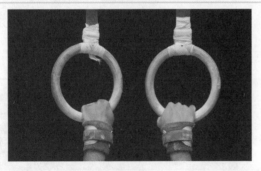

rose

rocket

rings

read

rabbit

rake

Check Understanding

By Regina Beau-

A. Listen. Complete the chart.

1. I know these words.	😊	😐	😞
2. I hear big ideas.	😊	😐	😞
3. I hear details.	😊	😐	😞

 Retell the story to a friend.

B. Show the order. Write 1, 2, or 3.

make food	plan	eat
☐	☐	☐

David Duck

D

d

desert

donkey

door

dishes

doll

dolphins

Writing

Listen. Look. Write.

Healthy food makes me _____.

Progress Check

A. Check the letter that matches.

		a	o	d
1.	O	☐	☐	☐
		R	T	P
2.	r	☐	☐	☐
		b	d	p
3.	D	☐	☐	☐
		F	L	T
4.	t	☐	☐	☐
		h	m	n
5.	H	☐	☐	☐

B. Review the letters.

What letter? What sound?

A o P t N s

Progress Check

Look at the picture. Check the word.

1.

☐ store
☐ breakfast
☐ set

2.

☐ make
☐ table
☐ food

3.

☐ table
☐ drink
☐ count

Animals All Around

The **BIG** Question

How are animals alike and different from each other?

☐ What animals live outside?

☐ What do animals eat?

☐ What animals are good pets?

93

About Animals!

1. What animals are on a farm?

pig

rooster

2. What animals are at the zoo?

lion

monkey

Can you name others?
Which do you like best?

3. What makes a good pet?

cat

dog

4. What can a pet do?

speak

cuddle

 Say **more!** Make a longer sentence. Use the word *and*.

dog

pet

speak

farm

rooster

pig

Pick an animal. Act it out!

zoo

lion

monkey

many

some

surprise

Turn and Talk Pick a word. Talk about it.

Paired Readings

Get ready to read.

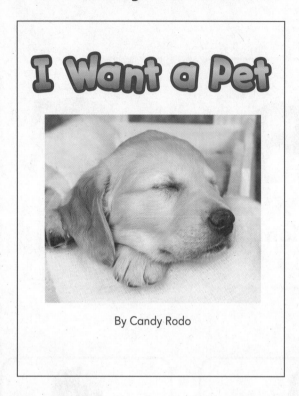

By Candy Rodo

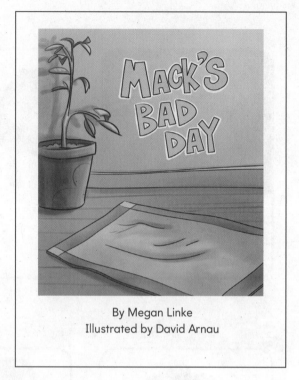

By Megan Linke
Illustrated by David Arnau

Flip through the books.
Talk about what you see.

Talk with a friend.
What is on the cover of *I Want a Pet*? And on the cover of *Mack's Bad Day*?

Check Understanding

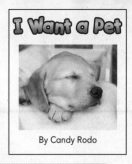

By Candy Rodo

A. Listen. Complete the chart.

1. I know about pets.	😊	😐	😞
2. I hear big ideas.	😊	😐	😞
3. I hear details.	😊	😐	😞

 Retell the story to a friend.

B. Look at the picture. Check the word.

1.

☐ Dad   ☐ dog

2.

☐ fish   ☐ pets

Umberto Umbrellabird

U

u

up

under

umpire

upside down

unzip

us

Word Work

A. Read the words.

1. p   a   n   pan

2. m   a   d   mad

3. f   a   n   fan

4. c   a   t   cat

Sight Words	that the too was

Talk About It   Use a sight word in a sentence.

B. Listen. Spell the word.

Check Understanding

By Megan Linke
Illustrated by David Arnau

Answer the questions.

1. Who is Mack?

☐   ☐

2. The cat got mad, so Mack ____.

sat   ran

☐   ☐

3. Mack had a ___ day.

good   bad

☐   ☐

Turn and Talk

Retell the story to a friend.
If you get stuck, ask for help.

Paired Readings

Get ready to read.

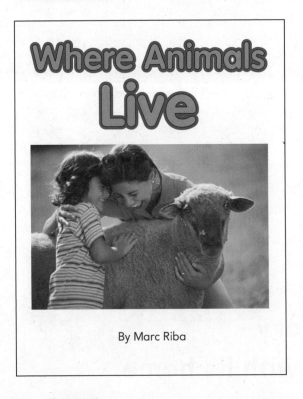

By Marc Riba

By Megan Linke
Illustrated by Pam López

Flip through the books.
Talk about what you see.

Talk about what you see on the covers of these books.

Check Understanding

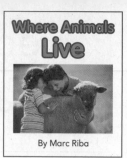
A. Listen. Complete the chart.

1. I know these words.	😊	😐	😞
2. I hear big ideas.	😊	😐	😞
3. I hear details.	😊	😐	😞

B. Think about the story.
Match the animal with its home.

1.

☐ zoo   ☐ farm

2.

☐ zoo   ☐ farm

Gabriel Goat

G   G

g   g

gopher

garden

guitar

gate

game

geese

Word Work

Read the words.

1. r   o   ck   rock

2. p   o   t   pot

3. f   o   g   fog

4. h   o   p   hop

Sight Words	he little

B. Write the words in the word family.

_____   _____   _____

- - - - - - - - - - - -   - - - - - - - - - - - -   - - - - - - - - - - - -

_____   _____

Felix T-Rex

box

mix

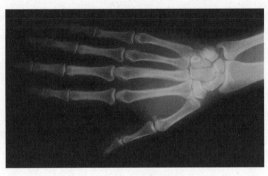

x-ray

fox

ax

six

Check Understanding

By Megan Linke
Illustrated by Pam López

Complete each sentence.

1.  Little Fox is on a ___.

log ☐   dog ☐

2.  Little Fox has to ___.

nap ☐   hop ☐

3. Little Fox got ___.

 ☐    ☐

Talk About It

Did you like the story?
Tell why, or why not.

Writing

A. What do animals like to do?
   Finish the sentence.

_____

- - - - - - - - - - - - - - - - - - - -

Some animals like to _____ .

B. Look at the pictures. Write about them.
   Use words you know.

Words I Know
chicken   hop   come   he   little   that
is   the   too   was   out   some   egg

Progress Check

A. Listen. Check the word.

1.	bad ☐	pad ☐	pod ☐
2.	log ☐	dog ☐	lad ☐
3.	pan ☐	fat ☐	pat ☐
4.	sad ☐	sod ☐	sob ☐

B. Review the letters.

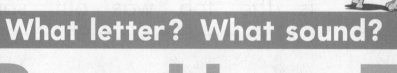

What letter? What sound?

R g U a T

Progress Check

Look at the picture. Check the word.

1.

☐ rooster

☐ zoo

☐ some

2.

☐ surprise

☐ monkey

☐ lion

3.

☐ pig

☐ dog

☐ zoo

Turn, Turn, Turn

The **BIG** Question

How do the seasons affect us?

☐ **What season is it now?**

☐ **Is it cold or hot?**

☐ **What do you do each season?**

About the Seasons!

1. When day turns to night, ___.

the sun sets

the moon rises

2. When months go by, ___.

the seasons change

I grow

3. Tell about the seasons.

In spring, I plant seeds.

In summer, it is hot!

In fall, it is cool.

In winter, it is so cold!

Say more! Find the mark: ,
Circle it.
How does it help you read?

year

summer

fall

season

winter

spring

Talk About It

Pick a word. Talk about it.

turn

night

day

moon

sun

month

Pick a word.
Draw a picture.

Yael Yak

Y y

yawn

yak

yogurt

yellow

yell

yarn

Paired Readings

Get ready to read.

What's in a
Year?

Today Is

4

Sat./Su
July

By Javier Sánchez

RAINY
DAY

By Megan Linke
Illustrated by Pam López

Read the titles.
Write words you know.

_____

- - - - - - - - - - - - - - - - - - -

_____

_____

- - - - - - - - - - - - - - - - - - -

_____

Talk
About
It

Talk about the covers.
Describe what you see.

Word Work

A. Read the words.

1. b   u   s   →   bus →

2. s   u   n   →   sun →

3. m   u   g   →   mug →

4. b   u   g   →   bug →

Sight Words	have into is of

B. Write the words in the word family.

_____   _____   _____

mug

Check Understanding

A. Listen. Complete the chart.

1. I know about years.	😊	😐	🙁
2. I hear big ideas.	😊	😐	🙁
3. I hear details.	😊	😐	🙁

B. Complete the sentence.

1.  A year has ____.

12 days ☐   365 days ☐

2.  A week has ____.

7 days ☐   52 days ☐

Check Understanding

By Megan Linke
Illustrated by Pam López

Look at the picture.
Check the words.

1.

   ☐ Tap, tap, tap

   ☐ Hop, hop, hop

2.

   ☐ Rub-a-dub-dub!

   ☐ Splash!

Talk About It

How does the kid in *Rainy Day* feel?
How do you know?

Isabella Iguana

I i

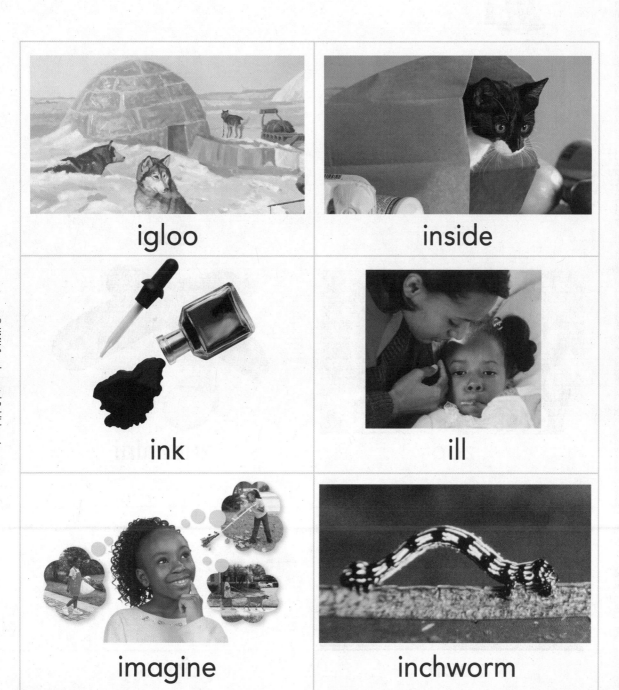

igloo

inside

ink

ill

imagine

inchworm

Zina Zebra

Z   Z

z   z

zip

zero

zoo

zucchini

zoom

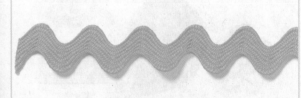

zigzag

Paired Readings

Get ready to read.

By Candy Rodo

By Megan Linke
Illustrated by Pam López

Turn and Talk Talk about the chart with a friend.

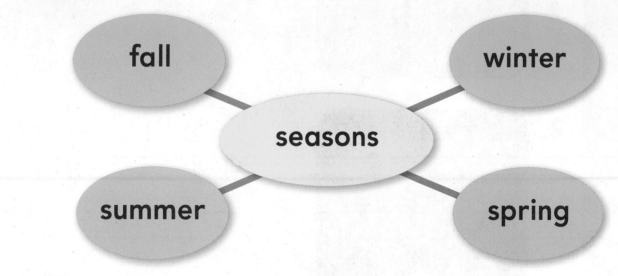

Talk About It What seasons do you see on the covers of these books?

125

Check Understanding

The Four Seasons

By Candy Rodo

A. Listen. Complete the chart.

1. I know these words.	☺	😐	☹
2. I hear big ideas.	☺	😐	☹
3. I hear details.	☺	😐	☹

B. Tell about the season.

1.

warmest   coldest

☐   ☐

2.

cool   gone

☐   ☐

Check Understanding

By Megan Linke
Illustrated by Pam López

Check the answer.

1. What does the girl have?

a fan ☐   a pan ☐

2. The sun is ____.

hot ☐   hat ☐

 Work with a friend. The word *it's* is made up of two words. What are they?

 How do you think the girl feels? How do you know?

127

Kyle Koala

 K

 k

kitten

kick

key

koala

kitchen

kite

Writing

A. Finish the sentence.

_____

- - - - - - - - - - - - - - - - - -

In the spring, I _____.

**B. Write about the picture.
Use words you know.**

Words I Know
into of is have spring season
day sun bug yum fun dog

Progress Check

A. Listen. Check the word.

1.	sun ☐	fun ☐	yum ☐
2.	lug ☐	dog ☐	lag ☐
3.	top ☐	tug ☐	gap ☐

B. Review the letters.

What letter? What sound?

i Y z K u

© HMH Supplemental Publishers Inc.

Progress Check

Look at the picture. Check the word.

1.

☐ night
☐ fall
☐ moon

2.

☐ winter
☐ summer
☐ sun

3.

☐ month
☐ winter
☐ spring

Growing Gains

The BIG Question

What happens when we grow?

☐ Are you taller or shorter than last year?

☐ How old are you now?

☐ What other things grow?

Let's Talk

About Growing!

1. A little baby is ___.

short

slow

2. A big kid is ___.

tall

fast

How have you changed?
How did you use to be?

3. A plant needs ___ to grow.

sunlight

water

4. A bud becomes ___.

a pretty flower

a fruit

 **Say more!** What else grows?
Use the word *and.*

grow

big

little

short

tall

fast

Get Moving

Pick a word.
Show what it means.

slow

water

sunlight

plant

flower

bud

Pick a word. Draw a picture.

Willie Wolf

web

wagon

watermelon

wink

wolf

worm

Paired Readings

Get ready to read.

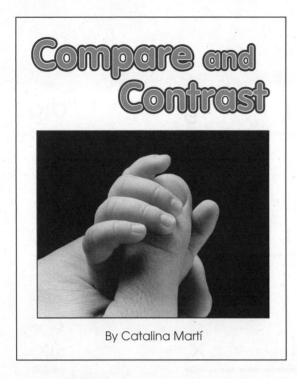

Compare and Contrast

By Catalina Martí

The Three Little Pigs

Traditional Tale
Illustrated by Moni Pérez

 **Ask a Teacher** What does it mean to compare?
If you don't know, ask a teacher.

Draw something big.
Draw something little.

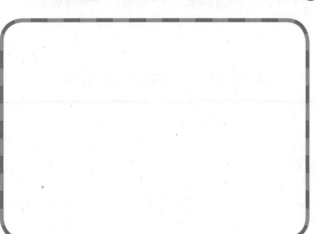

big   little

Word Work

A. Read the words.

1. d   i   g   →   dig →

2. b   i   b   →   bib →

3. s   i   x   →   six →

4. b   i   g   →   big →

Sight Words	me give eat let

Talk About It Use a sight word in a sentence.

B. Listen. Spell the word.

Check Understanding

A. Listen. Complete the chart.

1. I know about comparing.			
2. I understand the story.			

B. Which pair of pictures did we compare?

1.

☐   ☐

2.

☐   ☐

Check Understanding

Three Little Pigs

Traditional Tale
Illustrated by Moni Pérez

Complete each sentence.

1.

The pigs have to ____.

go ☐   stay ☐

2.

The wolf is ____.

small ☐   big ☐

Talk About It

How did the pigs feel at the beginning? How do you know?

Enam Elephant

E

e

elk

envelope

escalator

EXIT

exit

eggs

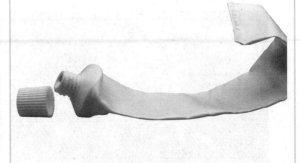

empty

Queen Quail

Q q

quarters

quilt

quartz

question

quarterback

quill

144

Paired Readings

Get ready to read.

By Emma Riba

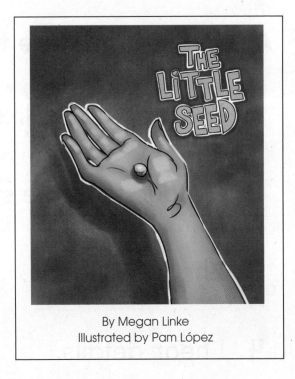

By Megan Linke
Illustrated by Pam López

Flip through the books.
Draw what you see.

 What do you know about seeds?
What do you know about flowers?

Check Understanding

By Emma Riba

A. Listen. Complete the chart.

1.	I've read books like this.	🙂	😐	😦
2.	I understand the story.	🙂	😐	😦
3.	I hear big ideas.	🙂	😐	😦
4.	I hear details.	🙂	😐	😦

 Retell the story to a friend.

B. Check the word.

1. Seeds need ____.

sunlight   buds

☐   ☐

2. Flowers grow ____.

little   tall

☐   ☐

Check Understanding

By Megan Linke
Illustrated by Pam López

Show the order. Write 1 or 2.

1.

2.

Retell the story. Use words you know.
If you get stuck, ask for help.

Jamila Jaguar

J j

jet

jam

jellybeans

jump rope

jar

jeans

Interview

Be very polite with teachers.
Be nice to friends and have fun, too!

Ask if anyone has a garden.
Make notes in the chart.

Ask a Friend	Ask a Teacher

Turn and Talk

Switch roles!
Let a friend ask you.

Writing

A. Finish the sentence.

_____

_ _ _ _ _ _ _ _ _ _ _ _ _ _ _

I used to _____.

B. Write about the picture.
Use words you know.

Words I Know

big bib me give
eat grow little

Word Families

Write words in the word family.

Letters to Use
b d r p f w

-ig

Progress Check

A. Listen. Check the word.

1.	kit ☐	quit ☐	fit ☐
2.	lip ☐	pin ☐	nip ☐
3.	fin ☐	fun ☐	fan ☐
4.	win ☐	wax ☐	man ☐

B. Review the letters.

What letter? What sound?

e W i J

© HMH Supplemental Publishers Inc.

Progress Check

Look at the picture. Check the word.

1.

☐ grow
☐ short
☐ water

2.

☐ sunlight
☐ bud
☐ fast

3.

☐ slow
☐ plant
☐ water

Away We Go

The **BIG** Question

How do people move from place to place?

☐ How do people move around?

☐ How do you go to school?

☐ What can you use to go faster?

About Going Places!

1. How do you go?

Do you go in a car?

Do you go on a bike?

Do you go on a bus?

Do you go on a train?

Where do you see this mark: ?
Why do we need it?

2. What rules do you know?

Stop.

Look.

Listen.

Follow the rules.

Read the rules.
How do the rules end?
☐ ?   ☐ !   ☐ .

Say more! Say a longer sentence.

ride

car

bike

careful

cross

bus

Pick a word. Draw a picture.

stop

look

listen

train

rules

safety

 Pick a word. Act it out.

Paired Readings

Get ready to read.

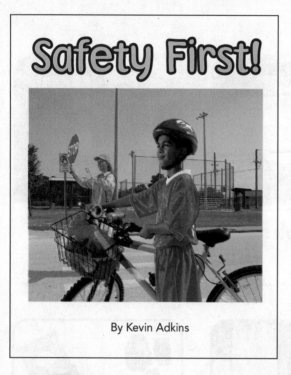

By Kevin Adkins

Traditional Tale
Illustrated by Eva Sánchez

Look at the stories.
Talk about what you see.

- Do you see  ?

- Do you see  ?

Talk with a friend.
What do you know about safety?

Check Understanding

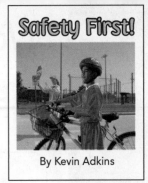

By Kevin Adkins

A. Listen. Complete the chart.

1. I've read books like this.	😊	😐	😞
2. I understand the story.	😊	😐	😞
3. I hear big ideas.	😊	😐	😞
4. I hear details.	😊	😐	😞

B. Answer the questions.

1.

How do you cross?

Walk!   Run

☐   ☐

2.

Where do you look?

left   both ways

☐   ☐

Word Work

A. Read the words.

1. s   e   t   →   set →

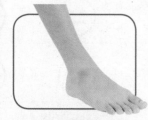

2. l   e   g   →   leg →

3. j   e   t   →   jet →

4. r   e   d   →   red →

Sight Words	get so

Talk About It

Talk about going places.
Use a sight word.

B. Listen. Spell the word.

_____

_ _ _ _ _ _ _ _ _ _ _ _ _ _ _ _ _ _

_____

Check Understanding

Check the answer.

1.

The girl is in ____.

red   yellow

☐   ☐

2.

The wolf ____.

eats grandma   runs away

☐   ☐

3. What is the title of the story?

The Bad Wolf   Little Red Riding Hood

☐   ☐

 Retell the story to a friend.
If you get stuck, ask for help.

 Work with a friend. What does
the -s in *eyes* tell you?

Vivian Vulture

V V

v v

vegetables

vine

violin

vet

volleyball

volcano

Paired Readings

Get ready to read.

Let's Go!

By Candy Rodo

THE BIG RACE

By Megan Linke
Illustrated by Pam López

Talk About It

Flip through the books.
Talk about who you see.

What are they doing? Draw a picture.

Check Understanding

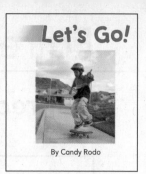

Let's Go!

By Candy Rodo

A. Listen to the story.
Complete the chart.

1. I know these words.	😊	😐	😞
2. I can understand the story.	😊	😐	😞

B. Match the picture with the word.

1.

boat ☐   bus ☐

2.

train ☐   car ☐

3.

boat ☐   bike ☐

Check Understanding

By Megan Linke
Illustrated by Pam López

Check the answer.

1. Who has a car?

Mel □   Ben □

2. Who has little legs?

Jess □   Buzz □

3. What is the title of the story?

The Big Race □   Mel □

Work with a friend. Find a question in the story. How can you tell it's a question?

Interview

 We speak differently to different people. Be very polite with teachers. Be nice to friends, and have fun, too!

Ask how people get to school.
Make notes in the chart.

Ask a Friend	Ask a Teacher

 Switch roles.
Let a friend interview you!

Writing

A. What will you do? Finish the sentence.

_____

- - - - - - - - - - - - - - - - - -

Tomorrow, I _____.

**B. Write about the picture.
Use words you know.**

Words I Know
for   go   leg   red
stop   look   listen
careful   cross   rules

Progress Check

A. Listen. Check the word.

1.	fed ☐	fell ☐	let ☐
2.	set ☐	sat ☐	sit ☐
3.	men ☐	man ☐	mom ☐
4.	wet ☐	vet ☐	vat ☐

B. Review the letters.

What letter? What sound?

Progress Check

Look at the picture. Check the word.

1.

- ☐ rules
- ☐ car
- ☐ train

2.

SCHOOL BUS

- ☐ bus
- ☐ stop
- ☐ rules

3.

- ☐ listen
- ☐ bike
- ☐ car

Acknowledgments

Text Acknowledgments:

© Advanced Assessment Systems, LLC/Linkit!. All rights reserved for all text on the following pages: 50, 52, 62, 65, 66, 67, 68, 70, 80, 83, 84, 85, 86, 88, 100, 101, 105, 106, 107, 118, 120, 123, 124, 128, 138, 140, 143, 144, 148, 162, 164

Illustration Credits:

All illustrations by Escletxa © Curriculum Concepts International

Photography Credits:

iii (bl) © SW Productions/Getty Images/Brand X Pictures; iii (backpack) HMH Co.; iii (elephant) © Digital Vision/Getty Images; iii (boy) HMH Co.; iv (butterfly) © Philip Coblentz/Brand X Pictures/ Getty Images; iv (ambulance) © Jupiterimages/Comstock Images/ Alamy; iv (sign) © PhotoDisc/Getty Images; iv (pizza) © John A. Rizzo/PhotoDisc/Getty Images; iv (t) © Digital Vision/Getty Images; iv (flowers) © Corbis Royalty Free; v (tr) Quinn Stewart/SV; v (bicycle) © Comstock/Getty Images; v (train) Don Couch/HRW Photo; vi (1) © FogStock/Alamy; vi (2) © Golden Pixels LLC/Alamy; vii (3) © Westend61 GmbH/Alamy; vii (4) Sam Dudgeon/HRW; viii (5) © Douglas Schwartz/Corbis; viii (6) © Jack Hollingsworth/PhotoDisc/ Getty Images; ix (7) © PhotoDisc/Getty Images; ix (8) HMH Co.; x (9) © DAJ/Getty Images; x (11) © Comstock/Getty Images; xi (13) © PhotoDisc/Getty Images; xi (15) © Peter Walker/Corbis; xii (17) © Mitch Hrdlicka/PhotoDisc/Getty Images; xii (19) © Stuart McCall/ Getty Images; xiii (21) HMH Co.; xiii (23) © Brand X/Jupiterimages; 30 (girl doing art) HMH Co.; 30 (teacher) HMH Co.; 30 (tr) © Jupiter Unlimited; 31 (school) HMH Co.; 32 © Getty Images; 32 (tl) HMH Co.; 32 (bl) HMH Co.; 32 (br) HMH Co.; 33 (girl with blocks) © Adobe Image Library/Getty Images; 33 (tr) HMH Co.; 33 (bl) © Jupiter Unlimited/Brand X Pictures; 33 (tl) HMH Co.; 36 (tr) HMH Co.; 36 (tl) © FogStock/Alamy; 37 (cr) HMH Co.; 37 (br) HMH Co.; 37 (cl) HMH Co.; 37 (bc) © Brand X Pictures/Getty Images; 37 (tr) © FogStock/Alamy; 37 (c) © FogStock/Alamy; 37 (bl) HMH Co.; 38 (cr) HMH Co.; 38 (cl) HMH Co.; 38 (br) © Corbis Royalty Free; 38 (bl) © SW Productions/Getty Images/Brand X Pictures; 39 (t) © FogStock/ Alamy; 41 (c) HMH Co.; 41 (br) HMH Co.; 41 (top) HMH Co.; 42 (boy with backpack) HMH Co.; 42 (tr) © Corbis Royalty Free; 42 (br) © Bananastock/Jupiter Images; 43 (c) © Digital Vision/Getty Images; 44 (bl) © Corbis Royalty Free; 44 (br) HMH Co.; 44 (tr) Ray Boudreau/HMH Co.; 44 (tl) © Weronica Ankarorn; 45 (eyes) HMH Co.; 45 (mouth) HMH Co.; 45 (tl) HMH Co.; 45 (tr) © Guy Jarvis; 48 (tr) Sam Dudgeon/HRW; 48 (tl) © Digital Vision/Getty Images; 49 (br) © Brand X Pictures/Getty Images; 49 (bc) © StockTrek/ PhotoDisc/Getty Images; 49 (eye) © Digital Vision/Getty Images; 49 (bl) © Digital Vision/Getty Images; 49 (elephant) © Digital Vision/

Getty Images; 49 (giraffe) © Westend61 GmbH/Alamy; 49 (tr) © Digital Vision/Getty Images; 50 (bl) HMH Co.; 50 (girl) © Creatas/Jupiter Images; 50 (tr) © Liquidlibrary/Jupiterimages; 50 (map) © Corbis Royalty Free; 50 (br) HMH Co.; 50 (tl) © Jupiter Unlimited; 51 (br) HMH Co.; 51 (sneakers) © Stockbyte/Getty Images; 51 (one sneaker) © Stockbyte/Getty Images; 51 (tr) Sam Dudgeon/HRW; 51 (bl) HMH Co.; 51 (br) HMH Co.; 52 (br) HMH Co.; 52 (salad) © Comstock/Getty Images; 52 (bl) © PhotoDisc/Getty Images; 52 (sunset) © Corbis Royalty Free; 52 (tl) © Corbis Royalty Free; 52 (tr) PhotoLink/PhotoDisc/Getty Images; 53 (c) HMH Co.; 55 (tl) HMH Co.; 55 (eyes) HMH Co.; 55 (bl) © Guy Jarvis; 56 (t) © PhotoDisc/Getty Images; 56 (c) © Corbis Royalty Free; 56 (b) Library of Congress; 56–57 HMH Co.; 58 (tl) H&S Graphics; 58 (tr) © Kent Knudson/PhotoLink /PhotoDisc/Getty Images; 58 (kitchen) Sam Dudgeon/HRW; 58 (bedroom) Sam Dudgeon/HRW; 58 © Jupiter Unlimited; 59 (t) © Emma Lee/Life File/PhotoDisc/Getty Images; 59 (c) © S. Solum/PhotoLink /PhotoDisc/Getty Images; 59 (b) © S. Solum/PhotoLink /PhotoDisc/Getty Images; 62 (tl) © Jupiterimages/Comstock Images/Alamy; 62 (tr) © Mitch Hrdlicka/PhotoDisc/Getty Images; 62 (cl) © Corbis Royalty Free; 62 (cr) © Westend61 GmbH/Alamy; 62 (bl) © Corbis Royalty Free; 62 (br) Digital Studios; 63 (tl) © Douglas Schwartz/Corbis; 63 (tr) © Jack Hollingsworth/PhotoDisc/Getty Images; 64 (t) © Douglas Schwartz/Corbis; 64 (house) © C. Borland/PhotoLink/PhotoDisc/Getty Images; 64 (kids) HMH Co.; 65 (tl) © Ellen Isaacs/Alamy; 65 (tr) © Stockdisc/Getty Images; 65 (cl) © Corbis Royalty Free; 65 (cr) © FPG International/Getty Images; 65 (bl) © Tetra Images/Alamy; 65 (br) © Digital Vision/Getty Images; 66 (tl) © Liquidlibrary/Jupiterimages; 66 (tr) © Artville/Getty Images; 66 (cl) © PhotoLink/PhotoDisc/Getty Images; 66 (cr) © Getty Images; 66 (bl) © John Coletti/Getty Images; 66 (br) © Corbis Royalty Free; 67 (tl) © Corbis Royalty Free; 67 (tr) © Alan and Sandy Carey/PhotoDisc/Getty Images; 67 (cl) © Jupiter Unlimited; 67 (cr) © Duncan Smith/PhotoDisc/Getty Images; 67 (bl) © Digital Vision/Getty Images; 67 (br) © Robert Glusic/PhotoDisc/Getty Images; 68 (tl) © Corbis Royalty Free; 68 (tr) © Jack Star/PhotoLink/PhotoDisc/Getty Images; 68 (cl) © Digital Vision/Getty Images; 68 (cr) HMH Co.; 68 (bl) © Corbis Royalty Free; 68 (br) © Corbis Royalty Free; 69 (t) © Jack Hollingsworth/PhotoDisc/Getty Images; 69 (crossing sign) HMH Co.; 70 (tl) © Ralph Lee Hopkins/National Geographic Stock; 70 (tr) © Comstock/Getty Images; 70 (cl) © Digital Vision/Getty Images; 70 (cr) © Corbis Royalty Free; 70 (bl) © Philip Coblentz/Brand X Pictures/Getty Images; 70 (br) © Comstock/Getty Images; 71 HMH Co.; 74 (t) © PhotoDisc/Getty Images; 74 (c) HMH Co.; 74 (b) © Corbis Royalty Free; 74–75 © PhotoDisc/Getty Images; 76 (tl) © C Squared Studios/PhotoDisc/Getty Images; 76 (tr) © Artville/Getty Images; 76 (bl) Victoria Smith/HRW Photo; 76 (br) © Comstock/Getty Images; 77 (tl) HMH Co.; 77 (tr) New England

Typographic; 77 (bl) HMH Co.; 77 (br) HMH Co.; 80 (tl) © Juniors Bildarchiv/Alamy; 80 (tr) © Corbis Royalty Free; 80 (cl) © Alan and Sandy Carey/PhotoDisc/Getty Images; 80 (cr) © PhotoDisc/Getty Images; 80 (bl) HMH Co.; 80 (br) Digital Studios; 81 (tl) © PhotoDisc/Getty Images; 81 (tr) HMH Co.; 81 (pepper) Kathryn Marlin/Rigby; 81 (eggs) HMH Co.; 81 (family) HMH Co.; 82 (grocery) © PhotoDisc/Getty Images; 82 (tl) © Corbis Royalty Free; 82 (tr) © PhotoDisc/Getty Images; 82 (bl) Sam Dudgeon/HRW; 82 (br) © PhotoDisc/Getty Images; 83 (tl) © Alamy Images Royalty Free; 83 (tr) © Corbis Royalty Free; 83 (cl) © Digital Vision/Getty Images; 83 (cr) © Corbis Royalty Free; 83 (bl) HMH Co.; 83 (br) © John A. Rizzo/PhotoDisc/Getty Images; 84 (tl) © Juniors Bildarchiv/Alamy; 84 (tr) John Langford/HRW Photo; 84 (cl) © Corbis Royalty Free; 84 (cr) © Corbis Royalty Free; 84 (bl) © C. Borland/PhotoLink/PhotoDisc/Getty Images; 84 (br) © Corbis Royalty Free; 85 (tl) © Corbis Royalty Free; 85 (tr) HMH Co.; 85 (cl) © D. Hurst/Alamy; 85 (cr) © Corbis Royalty Free; 85 (bl) ©Keith J Smith/ Alamy; 85 (br) © Ryan McVay/PhotoDisc/Getty Images; 86 (tl) © Corbis Royalty Free; 86 (tr) © Brand X Pictures/Getty Images; 86 (cl) © Rim Light/PhotoLink/PhotoDisc/Getty Images; 86 (cr) HMH Co.; 86 (bl) © Tony Fagan/Alamy; 86 (br) © Mitch Hrdlicka/PhotoDisc/Getty Images; 87 (t) HMH Co.; 87 (bl) © Ernie Friedlander/Cole Group/PhotoDisc/Getty Images; 87 (bc) HMH Co.; 87 (br) © Corbis Royalty Free; 88 (tl) © Corbis Royalty Free; 88 (tr) © Corbis Royalty Free; 88 (cl) Gary Russ/HRW Photo; 88 (cr) © Comstock/Getty Images; 88 (bl) Digital Studios; 88 (br) © Alamy; 89 © Javier Pierini/Digital Vision/Getty Images; 91 (t) © MIXA/Getty Images; 91 (c) © France & Symbols/Goodshoot/Jupiterimages; 91 (b) HMH Co.; 92 (t) © DAJ/Getty Images; 92 (c) © Photobon/Alamy; 92 (b) © Digital Vision/Getty Images; 92–93 © PhotoDisc/Getty Images; 94 (tl) © D. Falconer/PhotoLink/PhotoDisc/Getty Images; 94 (tr) © Digital Vision/Getty Images; 94 (bl) © Hogne Haug/Alamy; 94 (br) © Philip Coblentz/Brand X Pictures/Getty Images; 95 (tl) © Comstock/Getty Images; 95 (tr) © Comstock/Getty Images; 95 (bl) © Alamy; 95 (br) © Getty Images; 98 © DAJ/Getty Images; 99 (t) Don Couch/HRW Photo; 99 (b) © PhotoDisc/Getty Images; 100 (tl) HMH Co.; 100 (tr) HMH Co.; 100 (cl) © Corbis Royalty Free; 100 (cr) © Milton Montenegro/PhotoDisc/Getty Images; 100 (bl) HMH Co.; 100 (br) © Comstock/Getty Images; 101 (t) © Comstock/Getty Images; 101 (c) © Stockdisc/Getty Images; 101 (c) © D. Hurst/Alamy; 101 (b) © Artville/Getty Images; 103 (r) © Comstock/Getty Images; 104 (t) © Comstock/Getty Images; 104 (monkey) © face to face Bildagentur GmbH/Alamy; 104 (pig) © D. Falconer/PhotoLink/PhotoDisc/Getty Images; 105 (tl) © Digital Vision/Getty Images; 105 (tr) © Corbis Royalty Free; 105 (cl) © Jupiter Unlimited; 105 (cr) © PhotoDisc/Getty Images; 105 (bl) © SW Productions/PhotoDisc/Getty Images; 105 (br) © Digital Vision/Getty Images; 106 (t) © Siede Preis/

PhotoDisc/Getty Images; 106 (c) © Luminis/Alamy; 106 (c) © PhotoDisc/Getty Images; 106 (b) Victoria Smith/HRW; 107 (tl) © C Squared Studios/PhotoDisc/Getty Images; 107 (tr) Park Street Photography; 107 (cl) © Corbis Royalty Free; 107 (cr) © FPG International/Getty Images; 107 (bl) © Corbis Royalty Free; 109 (l) © Stockbyte/Getty Images; 109 (r) © LJSphotography/Alamy; 111 (t) © Digital Vision/Getty Images; 111 (c) © Hogne Haug/Alamy; 111 (b) © Ryan McVay/PhotoDisc/Getty Images; 112 (br) HMH Co.; 112 (tr) © SW Productions/Getty Images/Brand X Pictures; 112 (cr) © blue jean images/Getty Images; 113 © Ariel Skelley/Blend Images/Getty Images; 114 (br) © Comstock/Getty Images; 114 (tr) © Jupiter Images; 114 (bl) © Jupiter Unlimited; 114 (tl) © Jupiter Unlimited; 115 (bl) © Digital Vision/Getty Images; 115 (tr) © Getty Images; 115 (tr) ThinkStock/AgeFotostock; 115 (br) Matt Hind/Getty Images; 118 (tr) © PhotoDisc/Getty Images; 118 (tl) © Stockdisc/Getty Images; 118 (cl) © PhotoDisc/Getty Images; 118 (cr) © Corbis Royalty Free; 118 (bl) © D. Falconer/PhotoLink/PhotoDisc/Getty Images; 118 (br) © Photo objects.net/Jupiterimages; 119 (tr) © PhotoDisc/Getty Images; 120 (tl) © Comstock/Getty Images; 120 (sun) HMH Co.; 120 (mug) © Comstock/Getty Images; 120 (br) © G. K. & Vikki Hart/PhotoDisc/Getty Images; 122 (sunset) © Don Hammond/Design Pics/Corbis; 122 (bl) HMH Co.; 123 (bl) HMH Co.; 123 (girl) © Comstock/Getty Images; 123 (tl) Schawk; 123 (ink) © C Squared Studios/PhotoDisc/Getty Images; 123 (tr) © Comstock/Jupiterimages; 123 (br) © Getty Images; 124 (tl) © PhotoDisc/Getty Images; 124 (zoo) HMH Co.; 124 (zucchini) © Corbis Royalty Free; 124 (br) HMH Co.; 124 (bl) Comstock/Getty Images; 125 (tr) © Peter Walker/Corbis; 127 (bl) © Daniel Dempster Imaging/Alamy; 127 (bl) © Digital Vision/Getty Images; 128 (bl) HMH Co.; 128 (tr) HMH Co.; 128 (key) © Getty Images; 128 (br) © Ariel Skelley/Blend Images/Getty Images; 128 (koala bear) © Corbis Royalty Free; 128 (tl) Tetra Images/Getty Images; 129 (top) © Digital Vision/Getty Images; 132 (girl) Adobe Image Library/Getty Images; 132 (boy measuring) © Getty Images/Digital Vision; 132 (br) © Comstock/Getty Images; 133 HMH Co.; 134 (br) © Ariel Skelley/Blend Images/Getty Images; 134 (tr) HMH Co.; 134 (bl) © Comstock/Getty Images; 134 (tl) © PhotoDisc/Getty Images; 135 (tr) © Comstock/Getty Images; 135 (br) © PhotoDisc/Getty Images; 135 (tl) © Jupiter Unlimited; 135 (bl) © Emilio Ereza/Alamy; 138 (tr) HMH Co.; 138 (tl) © PhotoDisc/Getty Images; 138 (winking) © PhotoDisc/Getty Images; 138 (bl) © PhotoDisc/Getty Images; 138 (cl) © PhotoDisc/Getty Images; 138 (br) © Polka Dot Images/Jupiter Images; 139 (tr) © PhotoDisc/Getty Images; 140 (bl) © moodboard/Alamy; 140 (tl) © Corbis Royalty Free; 140 (bib) HMH Co.; 141 (car) Victoria Smith; 141 (car) Victoria Smith; 141 (bl) © Corbis Royalty Free; 141 (c) © Corbis Royalty Free; 141 (c) © Corbis Royalty Free; 141 (br) © PhotoDisc/Getty Images; 141 (skyscrapers) © PhotoDisc/Getty Images; 141 (tr) © PhotoDisc/

Getty Images; 141 (small building) HMH Co.; 143 (tl) © PhotoDisc/Getty Images; 143 (sign) © PhotoLink/Photodisc/Getty Images; 143 (bl) © PhotoDisc/Getty Images; 143 (cl) © Corbis Royalty Free; 143 (tr) © Getty Images; 143 (br) © Comstock/Getty Images; 144 (tr) Quinn Stewart/SV; 144 (cl) © Arkansas Dept. of Parks and Tourism; 144 (question mark) © Jupiter Unlimited/Thinkstock; 144 (br) © Corbis Royalty Free; 144 (bl) © Corbis Royalty Free; 144 (tl) © Artville/Getty Images; 145 (tr) © Stuart McCall/Getty Images; 147 (tr) © Stuart McCall/Getty Images; 148 (tr) © Corbis Royalty Free; 148 (cl) © PhotoDisc/Getty Images; 148 (bl) © Alamy Images Royalty Free; 148 (br) HMH Co.; 148 (tl) © Getty Images; 148 (jump rope) © PhotoAlto/Alamy; 150 (top) © PhotoDisc/Getty Images; 153 (tr) © Comstock/Getty Images; 153 (b) Stockbyte/Getty Images; 153 (c) © Jupiter Unlimited; 154 (t) HMH Co.; 154 (c) © Digital Vision/Getty Images; 154 (b) © Adobe Image Library/Getty Images; 154–155 © David R. Frazier Photolibrary, Inc./Alamy; 156 (tl) © Jupiter Unlimited; 156 (tr) © Comstock/Getty Images; 156 (bl) © Adobe Image Library/Getty Images; 156 (br) Don Couch/HRW Photo; 157 (tl) HMH Co.; 157 (tr) © Comstock/Getty Images; 157 (bl) Sharon Hoogstraten; 157 (br) © Blend Images/Alamy; 160 (tl) HMH Co.; 160 (c) Ruth Roman Brunke; 160 (b) HMH Co.; 161 (t) HMH Co.; 161 (c) © Blend Images/Alamy; 161 (b) HMH Co.; 162 (tl) © Comstock/Getty Images; 162 (cl) H&S Graphics; 162 (bl) © C. Lee/PhotoLink/PhotoDisc/Getty Images; 164 (tl) HMH Co.; 164 (tr) Sam Dudgeon/HRW; 164 (cl) © Creatas/Getty Images; 164 (cr) © Comstock/Getty Images; 164 (bl) © PhotoDisc/Getty Images; 164 (br) © Corbis Royalty Free; 165 (tr) © Brand X/Jupiterimages; 166 (t) © Adobe Image Library/Getty Images; 166 (c) © Bob Thomas/Alamy; 166 (b) © David R. Frazier Photolibrary, Inc./Alamy; 169 © Blend Images/Alamy; 171 (t) © Jupiter Unlimited; 171 (c) © Corbis Royalty Free; 171 (b) © Comstock/Getty Images.

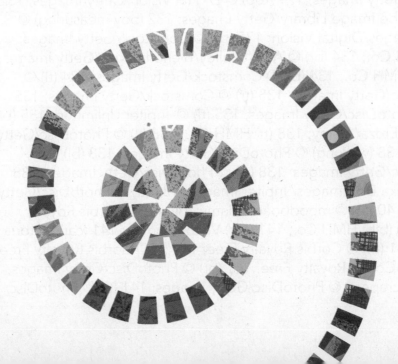

Story Photography Credits:

Story 1: 1 © FogStock/Alamy; 2 HMH Co.; 3 HMH Co.;4 © RubberBall/Alamy; 5 HMH Co.; 6 HMH Co.; 7 © PhotoDisc/Getty Images; 8 © Brand X Pictures/Getty Images. Story 2: 1 © Golden Pixels LLC/Alamy; 2 HMH Co.; 3 HMH Co.; 4 HMH Co.; 5 © Corbis Royalty Free; 6 © Brand X Pictures/Getty Images; 7 © SW Productions/Brand X Pictures/Getty Images; 8 © NASA - Headquarters - Great Images in NASA (NASA-HQ-GRIN). Story 3: 1 © Westend61 GmbH/Alamy; 2 © Westend61 GmbH/Alamy; 3 © StockTrek/PhotoDisc/Getty Images; 4 © StockTrek/PhotoDisc/Getty Images; 5 © Brand X Pictures/Getty Images; 6 © Brand X Pictures/Getty Images; 7 © Digital Vision/Getty Images; 8 © Digital Vision/Getty Images. Story 4: 1 Sam Dudgeon/HRW; 2 HMH Co.; 3 HMH Co.; 4 © Brand X Pictures/Getty Images; 5 © Stockbyte/Getty Images; 6 © Stockbyte/Getty Images; 7 HMH Co.; 8 HMH Co. Story 5: 1 © Douglas Schwartz/Corbis; 2 © C. Borland/PhotoLink/PhotoDisc/Getty Images; 3 © Douglas Pulsipher/Alamy; 4 HMH Co.; 5 © Alberto Fresco/Alamy; 6 © Kevin Burke/Corbis; 7 © Karl Kost/Alamy; 8 © Hisham Ibrahim/Photov.com/Alamy. Story 6: 1 © Jack Hollingsworth/PhotoDisc/Getty Images; 2 © PhotoDisc/Getty Images; 3 © PhotoDisc/Getty Images; 4 © Corbis Royalty Free; 5 © Corbis Royalty Free; 6 HMH Co.; 7 Library of Congress; 8 HMH Co. Story 7: 1 © PhotoDisc/Getty Images; 2 Sam Dudgeon/HRW; 3 © PhotoDisc/Getty Images; 4 © Corbis Royalty Free; 5 © PhotoDisc/Getty Images; 6 © Corbis Royalty Free; 7 Sam Dudgeon/HRW; 8 HMH Co. Story 8: 1 HMH Co.; 2 HMH Co.; 3 HMH Co.; 4 HMH Co.; 5 HMH Co.; 6 © Ernie Friedlander/Cole Group/PhotoDisc/Getty Images; 7 © Corbis Royalty Free; 8 © Corbis Royalty Free. Story 9: 1 © DAJ/Getty Images; 2 HMH Co.; 3 © Insy Shah/Gulfimages/Getty Images; 4 © Artville/Getty Images; 5 © DAJ/Getty Images; 6 © G. K. & Vikki Hart//PhotoDisc/Getty Images; 7 Don Couch/HRW Photo; 8 © PhotoDisc/Getty Images. Story 11: 1 © Comstock/Getty Images; 2 © Texas Department of Transportation; 3 © Corbis Royalty Free; 4 © Getty Images; 5 © Digital Vision/Getty Images; 6 © face to face Bildagentur GmbH/Alamy; 7 © Digital Vision/Getty Images; 8 © Photobon/Alamy. Story 13: 1 © PhotoDisc/Getty Images; 2 © Don Hammond/Design Pics/Corbis; 3 © Corbis Royalty Free; 4 HMH Co.; 5 © Ariel Skelley/Blend Images/Getty Images; 6 © Adobe Image Library/Getty Images; 7 HMH Co.; 8 © Joseph Sohm/Digital Vision/Getty Images. Story 15: 1 © Peter Walker/Corbis; 2 © Comstock/Getty Images; 3 © Getty Images; 4 © Daniel Dempster Imaging/Alamy; 5 © Digital Vision/Getty Images; 6 © Digital Vision/Alamy; 7 © Corbis Royalty Free; 8 © Digital Vision/Getty Images. Story 17: 1 © Mitch Hrdlicka/PhotoDisc/Getty Images; 2 © Corbis Royalty Free; 3 Victoria Smith; 4 © Tim Hall/PhotoDisc/Getty Images; 5 HMH Co.; 6 © Corbis Royalty Free; 7 © PhotoLink/PhotoDisc/Getty Images; 8 (horse) © G. K. & Vikki

Hart/PhotoDisc/Getty Images; 8 (cat) © Artville/Getty Images; 8 (parrot) © Stockdisc/Getty Images. Story 19: 1 © Stuart McCall/Getty Images; 2 © C. Borland/PhotoLink/PhotoDisc/Getty Images; 3 HMH Co.; 4 HMH Co.; 5 © DAJ/Getty Images; 6 © PhotoDisc/Getty Images; 7 © Bruce Heinemann/PhotoDisc/Getty Images; 8 HMH Co. Story 21: 1 HMH Co.; 2 © PhotoDisc/Getty Images; 3 HMH Co.; 4 © Blend Images/Alamy; 5 HMH Co.; 6 © Digital Vision/Getty Images; 7 HMH Co.; 8 HMH Co. Story 23: 1 © Brand X/Jupiterimages; 2 © PhotoDisc/Getty Images; 3 © Digital Vision/Getty Images; 4 © Bob Thomas/Alamy; 5 © David R. Frazier Photolibrary, Inc./Alamy; 6 © Corbis Royalty Free; 7 © Adobe Image Library/Getty Images; 8 © PhotoLink/PhotoDisc/Getty Images.

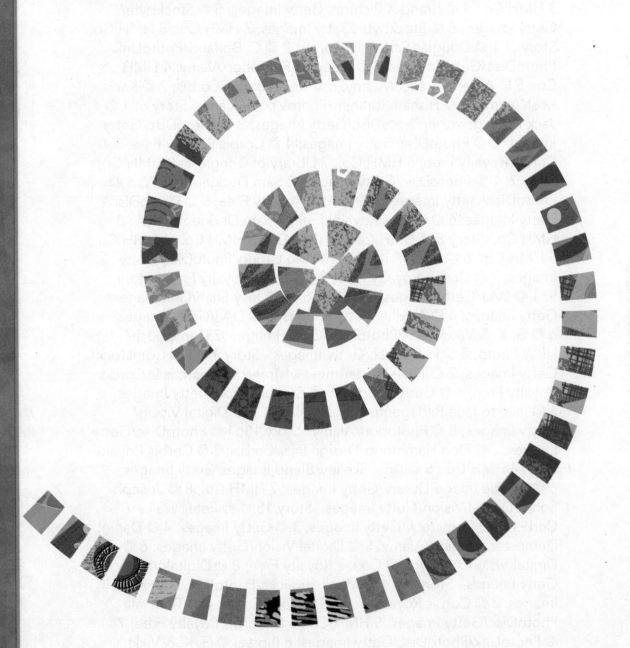

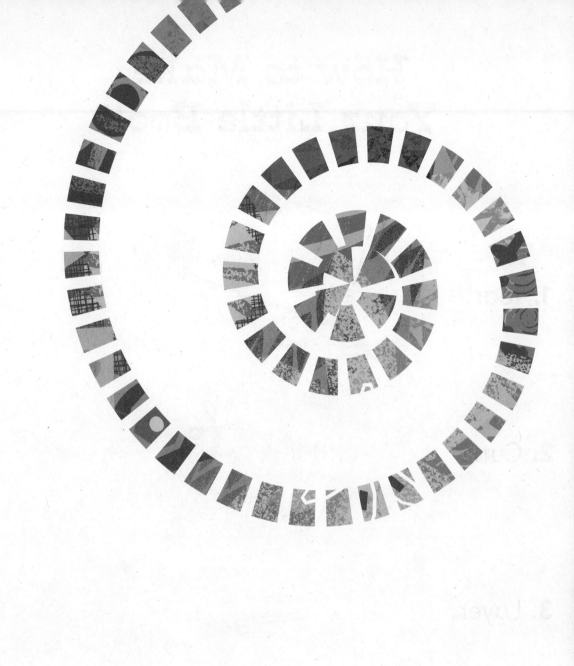

How to Make Your Little Book

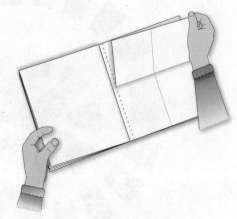

1. Tear.

2. Cut.

3. Layer.

4. Fold and staple.

5. Read!

Lex is fit.
He can run!

3, 2, 1, go!

Mel has a quick, red car.

Buzz has six little legs.

Who will win?

8

THE BIG RACE

By Megan Linke
Illustrated by Pam López

Jess has big, long legs.

6

Ben is set.
He has a jet.

3

Let's ride a bike!

How can you stay safe?

2

Let's ride on a bus!

What are the safety rules?

7

Let's ride on a train!

How can you stay safe?

4

Let's ride on a boat!

What are the safety rules?

5

Would you like to take a ride?
How can you stay safe here?

8

Let's Go!

By Eduardo Casas

Let's ride on this boat!
How can you stay safe?

6

Let's ride in a car!
What are the safety rules?

3

I am big.
I am bad.

2

Help!
You are no grandma.

7

I can get in.

4

Tap, tap, tap. Grandma!
I am in.

5

At last!
We are safe.

8

22

Little Red Riding Hood

Traditional Tale
Illustrated by Eva Sánchez

Your eyes are so big.
Your ears are so big.
Your teeth....

6

My red hood is on.
Grandma needs me.

3

What does the sign say?
Stop!

2

How can you help?
Leave helping dogs alone!

7

How do you cross?
Walk! Don't run.

4

Where do you look?
Look both ways!

5

Be careful!
Stop! Look! Listen!

8

Safety First!

By Kevin Adkins

What do you hear?
Listen for cars!

6

Where do you cross?
Find a crosswalk!

3

Dig, dig, dig.

Pick it.

Give it sun.

Let it sit.

Eat it.
Yum!

THE LITTLE SEED

By Megan Linke
Illustrated by Pam López

Up it comes!

Drop it in.

Pick a good spot.
Seeds need sunlight!

2

Flowers grow tall!

7

Water every day.

4

Look for seedlings!

5

Enjoy your garden!

8

Let's Grow Flowers!

By Emma Riba

Look for little buds!

6

Plant the seeds.

3

You are big!
Go! Go! Go!

No, Mama! No, no! No!
We are little.
We can not go!

2

I did it! I am in it!
No sticks!
I am in my house of bricks.

7

I can huff! I can puff!
I can blow the house in!

4

I did it! I am in it!
I am in my house of sticks!

5

The
Three Little Pigs

Traditional Tale
Illustrated by Moni Pérez

I can huff!
I can puff!
I can blow the house in!

I did it! I am in it!
I am in my house of straw!

This car is big!

This animal is slow.

These buildings are tall.

This building is short.

How are these animals alike?
How are they different?

8

Compare and Contrast

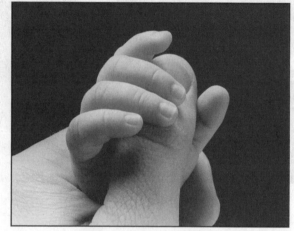

By Catalina Martí

This animal is fast.

6

This car is little.

3

The sun is hot.
Hot, hot, hot!

2

Have a nap in the sun.

7

Got a fan?

4

Buzz, buzz! A bug!

5

It's summer!

By Megan Linke
Illustrated by Pam López

8

A bit of fuzz!

6

Got a hat?

3

This is our Earth.
Where do you live?

2

A year has passed.
Summer is back!

7

Fall is cool.
See the leaves?

4

Winter is the coldest.
The leaves are gone.

5

Which season is next?

8

The Four Seasons

By Candy Rodo

In spring, grass grows.
Leaves return.

6

We have four seasons.
Summer is the warmest.

3

Tap, tap, tap.

2

Into the tub!

7

Hop, hop, hop.

4

Splash!

5

Rub-a-dub-dub!

8

By Megan Linke
Illustrated by Pam López

Mud. Yuck!

6

Bam!

3

A year has 365 days.
The sun is up!

2

A year has 12 months!

7

A year has 52 weeks.
Each week has 7 days.

4

A year has 52 weekends!
52 chances for fun!

5

Most years have 12 full moons!
What a year!

8

What's in a Year?

By Javier Sánchez

We play every day.
We play every week.

6

A year has 365 nights.
Day turns to night!

3

Little Fox got a log.

2

Hop, hop!

7

Not quite!

4

Little Fox got a rock.

5

Got it!

8

LiTTLE FOX

By Megan Linke

Illustrated by Pam López

He got on top.

6

He got on top.

3

Many animals live in zoos.

2

This pig lives on a farm.

7

Some lions live in zoos.

4

Many roosters live on farms.

5

What animal is this?
Where does she live?

8

Where Animals Live

By Marc Riba

Some monkeys live in zoos.

6

Some live on farms.

3

Mack had a mat.
Mack sat.

She had a nap.

A cat ran up.

That cat was mad!
Mack ran.

Too bad, Mack!

8

MACK'S BAD DAY

By Megan Linke

Illustrated by David Arnau

The cat sat on the mat.

6

Mack had a nap.

3

I want a pet!

2

"I have a surprise!"

Dad gave me a call!

7

I can get a cat!
No! Cats won't run with me.

4

I can get a dog!
Yes! A dog is a good pet.

5

What a surprise!
Two little pups!

8

I Want a Pet

By Candy Rodo

Woof!

Dogs can speak!
Dogs like to run!

6

I can get a fish!
No! Fish cannot speak!

3

© HMH Supplemental Publishers Inc.

How many will come?
Let's count!

2

Eat until you are full!

7

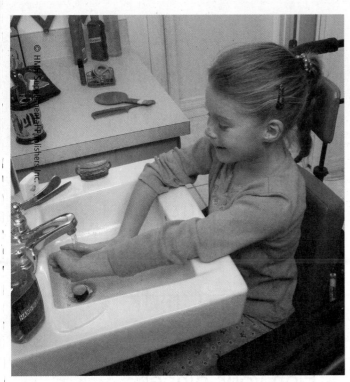

Wash up!

4

Set the table.
What do you need?

5

Then help clean up!

8

Please Come to Dinner!

By Regina Beaumont

Make the food.

6

Family Dinner Menu
grilled chicken
rice
peas and carrots
fruit salad
low-fat milk

Plan your dinner.

3

What a lot of food!

We eat fish for dinner.

We eat eggs for breakfast.

We drink a lot of milk.

It's time to check out!
It's time to go home!

Let's Go to the Store!

By Daniela Torres

We eat salads for lunch.

Start with a list!

I lost a triangle.
Help me find it.

2

This sign has my address.

7

Look at this sign.
Can you read it?

4

Look at this sign.
It names a street.

5

This is the best sign!
It is on the door of my room.

What Signs Say

By Jason Powe

This sign says to go slow!

I lost a circle.
Help me find it.

I lost a triangle!
Help me find it.

2

Look at this place.
Find a circle.

7

I lost some squares!
Help me find them.

4

Look at this place.
Find shapes here.

5

Look at this place.
What a lot of shapes!

8

Can You Find the Shape?

By John Wu

Look at this place.
Find two triangles.

6

I lost some circles.
Help me find them.

3

I put on my pants.

2

I grab my backpack!

7

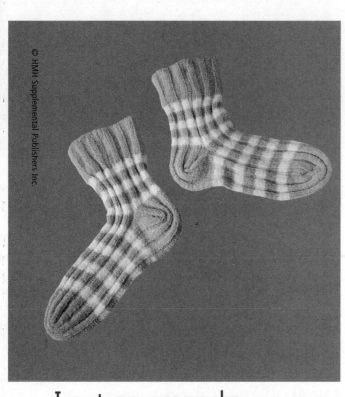

I put on my socks.

4

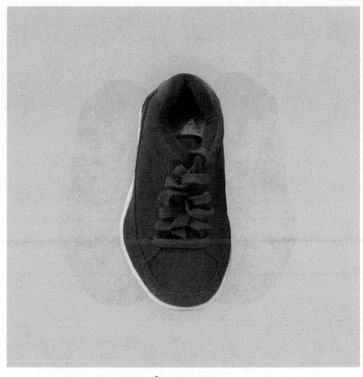

I put on one shoe.

5

This person is ready to go!

8

Time to Dress!

By Cristina Moreno

I put on the other shoe!

6

I put on my shirt.

3

This is a giraffe's eye!
Is it different from yours?

2

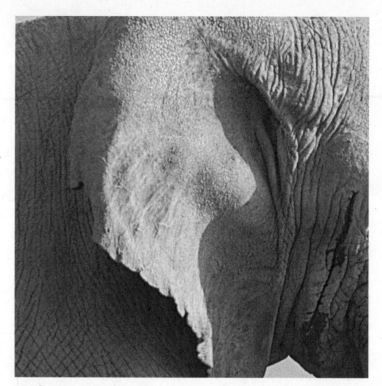

What is this?

7

This is a mandrill's nose!
How is it different?

4

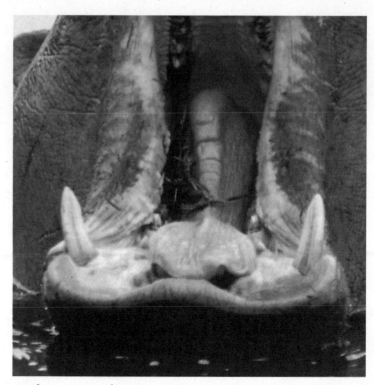

What is this?

5

This is an elephant's ear!
How is it different?

8

What Is This?

By Emma Riba

A big hippo mouth!
How is it different?

6

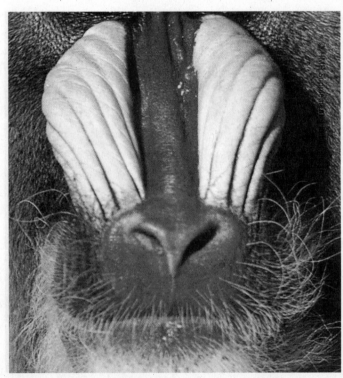

What is this?

3

This was my old school.

2

I am growing up!

7

I read new books.

4

I make new friends.

5

I can be anything!

8

Our Big Move

By Wendy Lee

I miss my old friends.

6

This is my new school.

3

First, we read books.

2

And tomorrow?

7

We can play.

4

We can color.

5

I wonder!

8

What Can We Do Today?

By Jason Powe

We can paint.

6

Then we can write.

3